Animal World
THE SQUIRREL

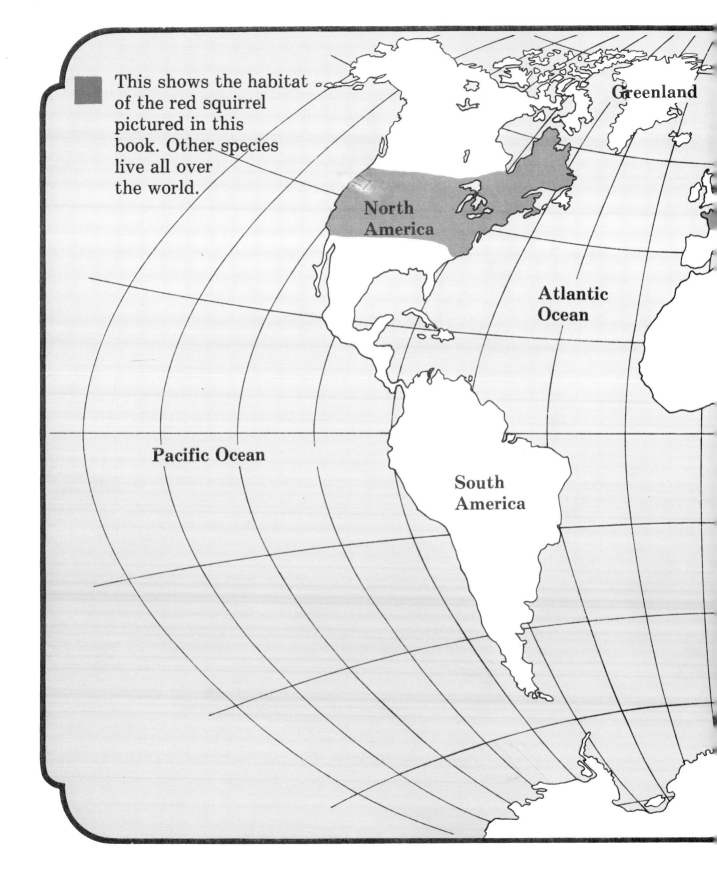

This shows the habitat of the red squirrel pictured in this book. Other species live all over the world.

Greenland

North America

Atlantic Ocean

Pacific Ocean

South America

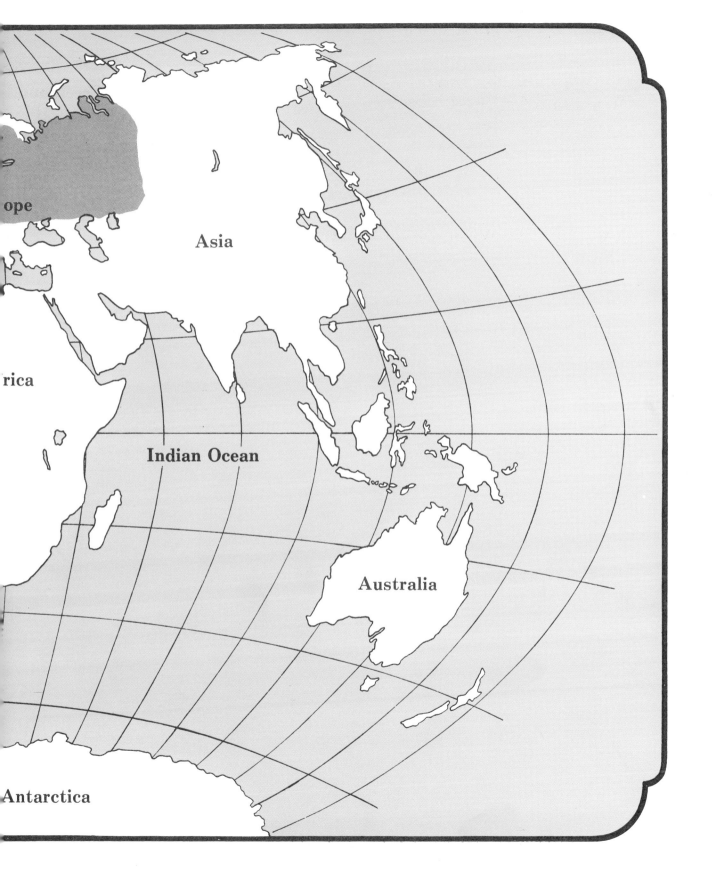

ope

Asia

rica

Indian Ocean

Australia

Antarctica

Published by The Rourke Enterprises, Inc., P.O. Box 711, Windermere, Florida 32786.
Copyright © 1983 by The Rourke Enterprises, Inc. All copyrights reserved. No part of this
book may be reproduced in any form without written permission from the publisher.
Printed in the United States of America.

Library of Congress Cataloging in Publication Data

Dalmais, Anne-Marie, 1954-
  The squirrel.

  (Animal world)
  Translation of: L'écureuil.
  Reprint. Originally published: London : Macdonald
Educational, 1978.
  Summary: Text and illustrations describe the physical
characteristics, habits, and natural environment of
the red squirrel.
  1. Eurasian red squirrel — Juvenile literature.
[1. Red squirrels.   2. Squirrels]   I. Oxenham, Patrick,
ill.   II. Title.   III. Series.
QL737.R68D3413   1984   599.3'232   83-9788
ISBN 0-86592-857-6

Animal World

THE SQUIRREL

illustrated by
Patrick Oxenham

ROURKE ENTERPRISES, INC.
Windermere, FL 32786

Looking for squirrels

Squirrels live deep in the forests where it is cool and dark. If you see half-eaten pine cones lying on the ground beneath fir trees, you can be sure that there are some squirrels not far away. Listen and watch for them.

Here in the fork of a tree, is the nest of some red squirrels. The picture shows it with the front cut away. Inside are the mother and three newborn babies. Their eyes will stay closed for about 30 days.

The squirrel family

It will soon be summer. The three young squirrels are now two months old, and they look very different. They now have fur which is reddish brown, and a white patch on the chest. They each have a graceful bushy tail and eyes sparkling with life.

The squirrels are now big enough to go out alone.

The three young squirrels give a dazzling display of leaping as they chase each other through the branches of a fir tree.

One of them gets tired of playing and settles down on a thick branch with a pine cone. He covers his back with his tail while he nibbles on the cone. He likes to eat the seeds inside it.

On another branch nearby, the mother is carefully combing her tail with her long, sharp claws. The father is not there. He has gone off to explore the forest.

The squirrel's nest

While the young squirrels are playing in the oak trees close by, their mother tidies up the nest.

The nest once belonged to a crow. The father and mother squirrels repaired and strengthened it. They made it ready for the birth of the young ones.

The nest is round in shape and made of twigs and leaves. It is lined with strips of bark and moss, and it has two entrances.

When they are about three months old, the young squirrels build their own nests.

Each squirrel marks out an area for itself. This is called its territory. The squirrel may build several nests inside it.

Keeping himself clean

The squirrel cleans his tail for a special reason. As long as his tail is really clean and light, he can use it as a parachute. If it is heavy with dirt and pine needles, it will not fluff up when he is in mid-air. The squirrel will then have a bad fall.

A young squirrel sits on the branch of a
tree and smooths his silky tail. He
lets the air puff it out. Then he jumps on
the trunk of the tree, climbs very quickly
to the top, and from there he leaps into
empty space. He glides splendidly. Thanks
to his marvellous tail, he can clear as
much as 65 feet in one jump. He lands
safely in a neighboring tree.

What squirrels eat

The squirrels scratch around on the ground to find food when they are hungry.

They especially like to eat acorns, beech nuts, chestnuts, walnuts, hazelnuts and the seeds from pine cones. They also enjoy wild berries, cherries, mushrooms, ants' eggs, and sometimes young birds.

One of the squirrels on the
previous page has found some
raspberries. Another nibbles a
mushroom. The squirrel on this
page has seen a large pine cone
lying on the forest floor. He
carries the cone away in his
mouth. Then he sits down at
the foot of a fir tree to eat the
seeds out of the cone in
comfort. Rolling it around
quickly in his nimble little
hands, he pulls the hard scales
off the outside. Using his sharp
teeth, he breaks up the cone
and finds the small, tasty seeds
that are hidden inside.

Many other animals live in
the forest. One of them is the
rabbit.

In danger and at play

The squirrel spends each night in one of his nests. During the day he wanders through the forest. He leaps from tree to tree, runs along the branches and scampers down the trunks.

He always has to be watchful, though, because some animals in the forest are his enemies. Martens are the worst. When a marten goes after a squirrel, the chase is fast and furious. The squirrel first lets out a gurgle of surprise. Then, he leaps on a birch tree and races up. The marten follows.

Hurling himself into empty space, the squirrel lands on another tree trunk and hides behind it. There he is safe from his enemy.

Luckily, squirrels do not often face such dangers. They are usually able to play their favorite games without being disturbed. In warm weather they like to find a stream and roll around in the damp moss. This is what the three squirrels in our picture are doing. They are having fun.

In the autumn

It is autumn. This is the time when the fogs roll in and the leaves fall from the trees. The hazelnuts fall too. Squirrels are very greedy about hazelnuts.

A squirrel opens a hazel nut with one neat bite. It is almost as if he had been taught how to go about it. He gnaws a groove in the shell and then cracks it open with his front teeth.

He collects several of these nuts. Then he settles down on a branch or tree stump to nibble them in peace.

If you see bits of broken hazelnut shells on the ground in a forest, look around for squirrels. You may not see them, but they are sure to be there.

Food stores for the winter

When the squirrels feel that winter is near, they begin to prepare for it. They gather acorns, seeds and hazelnuts. They put them into holes which they have dug in the ground, or under the moss. Sometimes they hide them between the roots of trees. They also collect mushrooms.

   The squirrels work hard. They will need a lot of food to keep them alive during the winter months.

Shelter for the winter

When the snow and frost come, squirrels take shelter in
their nests or in a hollow tree. The nest in the picture is
shown with the front part cut away so that you can see
how the squirrel curls up to sleep. Sometimes several
squirrels share the same shelter.

Some animals spend all of the winter sleeping. This is
called hibernating. Squirrels do not hibernate. Most
mornings they go for a short walk if the weather is not
too bad.

On these little trips they look for the food they have hidden away. When they come across the hiding place, they dig through the thick snow and bring up a nut. However, sometimes they forget where they have left the food. Then they have to return to their nests with nothing to eat.

Springtime again

In the spring everything in the forest wakes up. The squirrel goes running and jumping through the trees again. Everywhere there are new buds and shoots to eat.

Soon he chooses a partner and together they build a nest. The forest is becoming green again with new leaves. It won't be long before there are young squirrels to play in it.

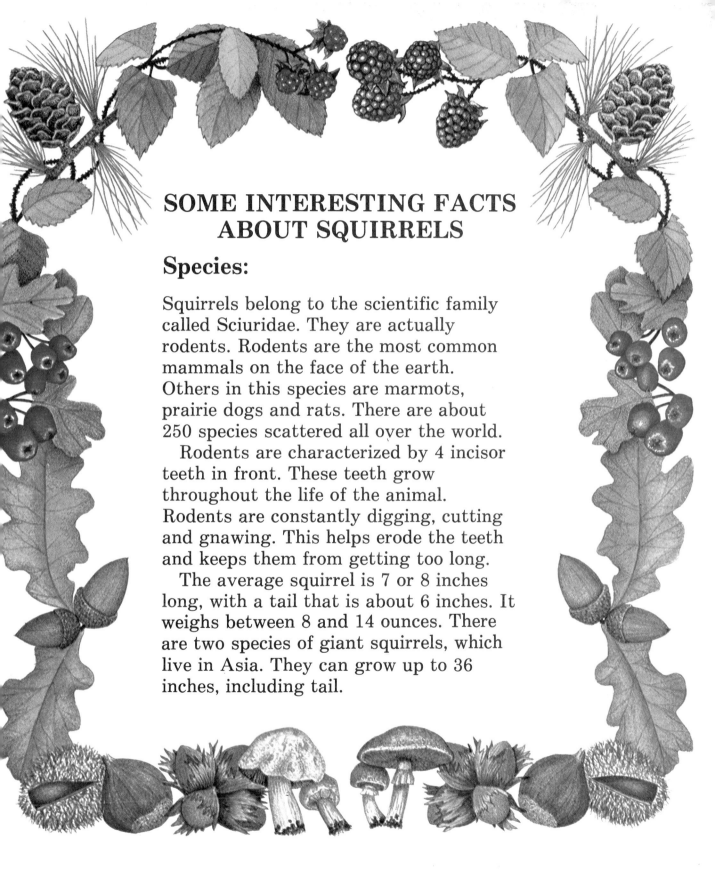

SOME INTERESTING FACTS ABOUT SQUIRRELS

Species:

Squirrels belong to the scientific family called Sciuridae. They are actually rodents. Rodents are the most common mammals on the face of the earth. Others in this species are marmots, prairie dogs and rats. There are about 250 species scattered all over the world.

Rodents are characterized by 4 incisor teeth in front. These teeth grow throughout the life of the animal. Rodents are constantly digging, cutting and gnawing. This helps erode the teeth and keeps them from getting too long.

The average squirrel is 7 or 8 inches long, with a tail that is about 6 inches. It weighs between 8 and 14 ounces. There are two species of giant squirrels, which live in Asia. They can grow up to 36 inches, including tail.

Description:

The most common squirrel is the grey squirrel. You
have seen it many times in parks and forests. It
originated in the eastern United States, but has spread
throughout Europe. It is especially common in England.
It was introduced there a number of years ago and has
become something of a pest. It seems that it has no
natural enemies in that country and so it has multiplied
rapidly. The grey squirrel loves to nibble on corn and
other crops and so it has become the farmer's enemy. It
lives in trees, making its nest in the knotholes. It
spends a lot of time on the ground, though. It is always
looking for food.

The red squirrel, or chickaree, is the one pictured in
this book. It can be found from coast to coast in the
cooler areas. It is also found in northern Europe. The
dusty Douglas and pine squirrel are very similar to the
red. Their color is very pretty and they are rather tidy
eaters. You can always tell where a red squirrel has
eaten because it leaves behind a neat pile of nut shells
and cones.

There is a species of squirrels called the "flying
squirrel." Of course, they do not actually fly. What they
do is glide. They jump from a tree with all four legs
spread out. They have a web of skin between their legs
that looks like a parachute. This enables them to glide
gently to the ground. The Northern flying squirrel likes
to live in evergreens. There is also a southern species.

Ground squirrels dig burrows for their homes. They are cute and fluffy but one should approach them with care. They are usually infested with ticks and fleas. In fact, they carry some very serious diseases. They can transmit spotted tick fever and relapsing fever, both can be fatal to human beings. An example of a ground squirrel is the golden-mantled squirrel. It is one of the few which sports a bright coat of fur. It has orange stripes on its back. However, most ground squirrels are quite dull in color.

Tree squirrels live on every continent, except Australia. As the name implies, they build their nests in trees. In the winter they will live in a knothole of a tree. In the summer they make a nest of leaves and twigs in the fork of a branch of a tree. The flying squirrel is a tree squirrel. So is the fox squirrel of New England.

Tree squirrels have an interesting way of coming down from a tree. They descend head first. Most humans would find this a frightening thing to do. However, it does not seem to bother them. They can often be seen running up and down trees with some nuts or other goodies tucked in their mouth pouches.

Squirrels have bushy, furry tails which measure almost as long as their bodies. They use their tails for balance during their jumps. It is very important that the squirrel keep its tail clean. A tail which is dirty will cause the squirrel to fall in flight.

Family Life:

As we said before, there are ground squirrels and tree squirrels. Ground squirrels are some of the best engineers and construction experts in the animal world. Remember, they are cousins of the beaver. They do not build as elaborate a home as the beaver. However, they are impressive. The tree squirrel makes a nest 18 inches wide and lives inside the tree when it grows cold. You can see the summer nests easily in winter when all the leaves have fallen.

Ground squirrels eat mostly plants. The Northern flying squirrel is an exception. It slips into bird feeding stations at night. There it will eat bird eggs, young birds, insects and tree buds. Another favorite food is corn. A squirrel will eat the germ end of the corn kernel and leave the rest. If a squirrel wants to store food in a safe place, it will hold it in its mouth pouch and bury it in the ground or take it back to the nest. Often squirrels will forget where they planted their nuts. This is lucky for the forests. Every planted nut is a new tree.

Squirrels are very sociable creatures. They can be seen chasing each other up and down trees. They like to play. In parks, they will come up to people and ''beg'' for food.

They are great jumpers. This is due to their strong leg muscles and their tails. A grey squirrel, measuring only one foot long, can jump four feet.

Conservation:

Squirrels do not really have a conservation problem.
They are numerous in most of the areas which they
inhabit.

They must always be on the lookout for cats and birds
of prey, like hawks. These animals consider squirrel a
very good dinner.

Like all other animals, squirrels are dependent on the
food supply. The population builds when food is
plentiful. Sometimes the crops fail or the winter is very
cold. There may be little food. When faced with this
problem the squirrel will emigrate. That means that it
will leave its home to find a place that has a more
plentiful food supply. When it is found, the squirrel will
not return home. There have been several mass
movements of squirrels in the Midwest and Northeast.
Grey squirrels have been known to swim across rivers in
the thousands to reach food on the other side.